The FACT ATTACK series

FACT ATTACK

NUTTY NUMBERS

ROWLAND MORGAN

MACMILLAN CHILDREN'S BOOKS

First published 1998 by Macmillan Children's Books

This edition published 2012 by Macmillan Children's Books
a division of Macmillan Publishers Limited
20 New Wharf Road, London N1 9RR
Basingstoke and Oxford
Associated companies throughout the world
www.panmacmillan.com

ISBN 978-1-4472-2431-0

1 3 5 7 9 8 6 4 2

A CIP catalogue record for this book is available from
the British Library.

Printed and bound by CPI Group (UK) Ltd, Croydon CR0 4YY

UNITS

To express today's huge statistics in a way that is easier to picture than strings of figures, we use big visual units. Here's a list of the main ones with their facts and figures.

SUPERTANKER

Load: 100,000 tonnes
The world fleet of supertankers is approximately 800. Three thousand smaller tankers have a combined cargo capacity of 263 million tonnes. The total tanker fleet capacity is about 360m tonnes.

JUGGERNAUT LORRY

Average load: 44 tonnes
16.5 metres long
There are 94,000 articulated lorries in Britain. They could jam up a six-lane motorway for 270 kilometres, or 168 miles, further than London to Birmingham. They can carry between 20 and 24 tonnes of freight.

Road Tanker
Capacity 34,000 litres/7,478 gallons

Jumbo Jet
350–450 passengers
Cruising speed: 600 ground mph
Cruising altitude: 49,000 feet

Airship
105,000 cubic metres of gas/3,700,000 cubic feet

Hot Air Balloon
2,180 cubic metres/77,000 cubic feet. The air in a Montgolfier hot air balloon of the "77" championship type weighs between three and four tonnes.

Busload
50 people

Titanic
52,250 tonnes
2,435 people

Eiffel Tower
300 metres high
8,757 tonnes

Great Pyramid of Cheops
Weight: 7,000,000 tonnes

Power Station
2,000 megawatts/2 gigawatts

Olympic Swimming Pool
Capacity: 2,300 cubic metres
(2,300,000 litres/506,000 gallons)

Round the World
40,075 kilometres/24,902 miles

Earth to the Moon
382,000 kilometres/237,000 miles (average)

DID YOU KNOW THAT . . .

1 One-third of the world's population are children.

8 The National Lottery is estimated to have created between 10 and 12 million new shopping trips a year.

1 UK builders use 20 times more wood than Britain can provide.

8 At its 50 per cent recycling target, the aluminium drinks can business will still be dumping 3.25 billion cans a year on to the British landscape, or over 6,000 a minute. Recycling just one aluminium drinks can is the equivalent of keeping a 100w light bulb burning for 4 hours.

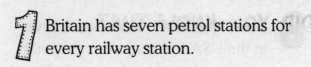

1 Britain has seven petrol stations for every railway station.

8 A year's cars produced in Europe could easily queue round the world.

1 The money spent on adverts for toys and games could pay for nearly half the year's school books.

8 Swedes spend more than twice as much as Britons on books, newspapers and magazines.

1 You could stand the world population in the state of Texas.

8 Each trout in the Yellowstone River in the USA's Yellowstone national park is estimated to be caught 10 times during the fishing season.

1 The Swiss eat three times as much beef as the British.

8 Of every mile travelled by an average person, only 10 yards is by bike.

1 A grower could use a different pesticide product every day for over eight years.

8 An airliner could taxi 90 miles along Heathrow Airport runway approaches.

6

1 On average, 71 attempts to hack into the computer system of the Pentagon (the headquarters of the US defence forces) are successful every day.

8 There are 2.2 chickens for every person in Britain.

1 Toyota's 40 million-watt Burnaston car plant could light 160,000 homes.

8 30,000 litres of water are polluted to process the components of one new car.

1 There are 3,596 cinema screens in Britain, 4,821 in France and 41,000 in the USA.

8 Over 70 per cent of Colombia is covered by forest, and seven per cent of Britain.

1 There are 255,000 mopeds in Britain and 14 million in Japan.

8 There are 13 French nuclear power reactors within 85 miles of the British coast.

1 There are 4,709 radio stations in Italy.

8 There are 36 million sheep and lambs in Britain.

1 In the USA, 350 slices of pizza are consumed every second.

8 There are over 111 million head of cattle on North American farms.

1 There are 155,333 post offices in India, meaning you could visit a different one every day for 425 years.

8 There are 854 bookshops in South Africa and 78,186 in Japan. (That's one bookshop for every 49,000 people in South Africa, and one for every 1,600 in Japan.)

1 There have been 3,000 sightings of UFOs by military and civilian pilots.

8 You control 11,000 moving parts of your body.

1 About 10,000 smells are recognized by the human nose.

8 You spend an average of 23 years asleep in a 70-year human life.

1 There are nearly two football fields of world farmland per person.

8 Some 50 million tribal people still live in the tropical rainforests.

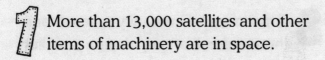 More than 13,000 satellites and other items of machinery are in space.

8 There are 4 million jumbo-jetloads of children in the world.

1 The estimated population of ancient Rome was 600,000; the estimated population of the 'Bosnywash' (Boston-New York-Washington) urban area in the USA is 45 million.

8 The average American drinks about half a bathful of soft drinks a year.

1 A quarter of a million huge blue whales were roaming the oceans in the pre-industrial era, compared to about 5,000-12,000 today.

8 Time taken by humanity to reach one thousand million population: 3 million years.

1 Additional time taken by humanity to reach two thousand million population: 100 years.

8 Additional time taken by humanity to reach three thousand million population: 30 years.

1 Additional time taken by humanity to reach four thousand million population: 15 years.

8 There are more head of cattle on Earth than people in China.

1 Americans eat 14 supertanker cargoes of biscuits per year.

8 Humans have eaten about 7,000 different types of plant in history. There are 75,000 available.

1 There may be as many as 80 million different species of life on Earth.

8 Only seven per cent of the world's land is covered by tropical forest.

1 It takes 200 BTUs (British Thermal Units) of energy to make a glass pop bottle used 10 times, and 7,000 BTUs of energy to make one aluminium pop can used once.

8 Over 105 million bicycles are produced per year worldwide.

1 Fewer than one person in 10 in the world owns a car.

8 There are over 85,000 dams in the USA.

1 There are at least 100,000 electrical power stations in the world.

8 A typical train holds 1,400 passengers. The equivalent number of car passengers would take up 20 miles of road.

1 About 170 cars per day are sold at one dealership, Ed Morse Chevrolet Inc, Lauderhill, Florida, USA.

8 It takes a century for a mature tree to produce the oxygen consumed by a car going 18,000 miles at 30 miles per gallon.

1 25 billion sets of throw-away chopsticks are used each year in Japan.

8 Rockets launching satellites have ripped a gash in Earth's protective ozone layer on average once every four days since 1957.

1 For every two lorries driving through German neighbourhoods, there are three in Britain.

8 There has been a 50% increase in the number of operations performed on the NHS in the past ten years.

1 The average daily number of low-flying warplane sorties over peacetime Britain is 436.

8 On any day, only one car in 13,000 gets stolen.

 25,000 Barbie dolls sell per business hour.

8 One in five British buses are defective.

1 Britons have half as many computers as Americans, and 134 times more than Indians.

8 England's King Edward II spent enough on wine in one year to employ 6,666 ploughmen.

1 In the UK, four weddings and a funeral would cost on average £79,000, or nearly three years' average pay.

8 Domestic freezers sold every year in Britain would stack 112 times higher than Mont Blanc.

1 A coal-fired power station wastes two-thirds of its energy.

8 The British population is expected to increase by 10 busloads a day.

1 To design their new plane, Boeing engineers could have used a different computer terminal every working day for eight years.

8 The world's fishing fleets cost nearly twice as much as their catch.

1 Japan has twice as many industrial robots as the rest of the world put together.

8 Each minute of *The Last Action Hero*, starring Arnold Schwarzenegger, lost Columbia Pictures nearly a million dollars.

1 Between being caught and causing the first sneeze, a cold virus multiplies its number by about ten thousand million fold.

8 The Beatles' performing fee multiplied by 80 times in a year.

1 You are at least 65 per cent water.

8 Notorious Wild West frontier towns had 1,000 times fewer murders and woundings than Los Angeles today.

1 The mouth of a recently-designed Icelandic trawling net is large enough to trap 12 jumbo jets in piles six high at the same time.

8 The Black Sea has been given between 3,650 and 5,475 days to live.

1 A gas-fired power station wastes over half of its energy.

8 Fun-loving tourist destination Miami, Florida, wastes as much water in one day as the entire US state of Maine drinks in a year.

1 The equivalent of 20,000 manuscripts the length of *War and Peace* is sent by American electronic mail every day.

8 Making daily trips, a keen hydrologist would need 205 years to visit all the USA's dams.

1 Even travelling at the speed of light, it would take 1,300 years to reach the first known planet outside our solar system.

8 Indonesia has banned 57 out of the 63 pesticides polluting its land and food.

1 Japanese roads could pave the state of Luxembourg four times.

8 Only 10 per cent of humans can afford to buy a car, while 80 per cent can afford a bike.

7 President Obama could grant an interview to a different White House correspondent every working day for six years.

8 Half the earth's surface is three kilometres or more below sea level.

1 The average American golf course uses enough water to supply the needs of between 2,000 and 11,000 people.

8 About 30,000 white birch trees were felled to make tees in use by US golfers.

1 Rich countries have about 24 times more blood for transfusion than poor ones.

8 Dhaka (the capital of Bangladesh) has an estimated 400,000 rickshaw pullers.

1 The number of tourists flying over the Grand Canyon has doubled during the last five years.

8 A sports team could play on a different Greater London playing field every Saturday for 100 years.

1 Every minute, Americans eat 10,000 trays of a dozen eggs, or a stack as high as the Empire State Building in New York.

8 Americans eat 12 Olympic swimming poolfuls of popcorn a day.

1 Italians eat 43 times more shellfish than Britons.

8 A German spends nearly twice as much on food as a Briton.

1 The average American woman owns five pairs of sunglasses.

8 The Prime Minister uses half a million pounds' worth of car transport a year.

1 The Channel Tunnel reduces freight time to southern Europe by only seven minutes an hour.

8 Every working day, British diplomats spend over £27,000 entertaining.

1 Thirteen of the 14 Concorde supersonic airliners previously in service were operating six to eight years beyond their original design life!

8 Nearly 1,000 of Britain's bridges are being strengthened to bear the weight of 40-tonne juggernauts.

1 Eight different waste bins are required in Swedish households by law – for metals/plastics, paper/cardboard, glass, newspapers, aluminium cans, plastic bottles, glass bottles and rubbish.

8 When Denmark played France 'A' in the 1908 Olympics, a goal was scored on average every five minutes.

1 Tennis legend Ivan Lendl has earned $1,500 for every day he has been alive, but Steffi Graf has earned over $1,700.

8 In 25 years, more people will have been added to the world population than were alive in 1933.

1 Rubbish-dump scavengers in Recife, Brazil, collect 120 tons of materials a day for recycling.

8 Nine out of 10 recognizable names given by 20m Internet computer network users are male.

1 It would take 12 sets of the *Encyclopedia Britannica* to hold the 300 billion "letters" of one person's genetic profile.

8 Two per cent of the final cost of a British-sold banana goes to the workers on overseas plantations.

1 Mowing the lawn with a petrol mower for one hour produces the same amount of smog components as driving a car 18.6 miles.

1 Researchers found 476 items of manufactured rubbish per hour on an uninhabited Pitcairn Islands beach 5,000 km from anywhere in the Pacific.

8 China aims to keep its acid-rainmaking sulphur dioxide emissions to three supertanker-loads a week.

1 About 83 juggernaut-loads of clothes, curtains and other textiles a day are thrown on British rubbish dumps.

8 Farting farm animals could be causing up to a fifth of a major global-warming gas.

1 New York City has nearly as many children in foster care as the whole of England.

8 Aerosols emerging from UK factories each working day could be littered nose-to-tail along the road from Plymouth to Newcastle.

1 Far from falling, child fares on London's public transport are set to have actually doubled within the span of one childhood.

8 The odds are stacked 188,405-to-1 against winning the £10,000 prize on a single ticket in the British state lottery. 1 in 13,983,816 people win the National Lottery.

1 The Indian sub-continent's tiger population is one-thirteenth what it was 60 years ago.

8 At least 21,000 personnel were physically close to British atom bomb tests.

1 Played continuously on one channel, British TV commercials booked to sell the video version of *Jurassic Park* would last more than 18 working weeks.

8 Bus lines pay at least four times more for fuel than airlines.

1 Africa may contain twice as much wood as previously believed.

8 If drivers divide their mileage driven by the time they spend working to buy, driving, repairing, cleaning and otherwise attending to their car, they actually motor at an average speed slower than a horse.

30

1 One book page devoted to describing each species of life on earth would fill 6 km (3.75 miles) of bookshelf.

8 A year of Europe's junked aerosol cans could easily stack to the moon.

1 If paid his 1993 earnings in compact discs, Thorn EMI's head of music would have received a stack of CD recordings higher than Mount Everest. Thorn EMI was disposed of in 2007.

8 Since 1960 an estimated six million dolphins have died as a result of tuna fishing for the UK and USA.

1 An average Briton born today can expect to watch TV for 11 solid years in their lifetime.

8 Not a single river in the USA is safe to drink from or swim in.

1 Drivers cause nearly as many serious injuries to non-drivers as they do to themselves and other drivers.

8 An estimated four million boys and girls were sacrificed by the Aztecs.

1 Sixty-eight times more is spent advertising cars than trains in national newspapers.

8 The world's fishing fleets now throw away more sea-life than they used to catch.

1 The largest mammal is 70 million times bigger than the smallest.

8 China's medicine trade could wipe out all wild tigers in eight years.

1 The world's whole supertanker fleet would not be able to deliver a year's worth of newspapers to the USA.

8 2.4 books in Welsh are published per working day.

1 About 108,000 average lifetimes could pass during a year's British TV viewing.

8 A Javan rhinoceros is almost as rare as a painting by the Dutch master Vermeer.

1 Nearly three-quarters of Earth's surface is water and nearly a third of the land surface is desert.

8 On average, more than 19 chemical spills, explosions and other accidental toxic releases are known to occur each day in the USA.

1 TV owners spend more on pay-to-view TV films than cinema fans do on films shown at the cinema.

8 Every living tonne of shark requires at least a thousand tonnes of microscopic phytoplankton.

1 A glass of bottled mineral water costs 15,000 times more than a glass of tap water.

8 Four out of five new aluminium cans are dumped on the landscape.

1 An average Ghanaian spends US $5 a year in the shops; a Japanese person: US $9,000.

8 North Americans use 300 times more petrol than residents of India.

8 Between 1945 and 1976, 25 million people died in 133 wars.

1 Residents of Sussex lived without cars for nearly 20,000 generations.

8 The Soviet state used atomic bombs as excavators 116 times.

1 Between 1780 and 1880 an estimated seven million acres of common land was seized by private property owners.

8 Satellites show more than 10,000 kilometres of British hedgerow disappeared completely between 1990 and 1993.

36

1 Americans bin more than 10 supertankers of paper a week.

8 A heavy object dropped into the ocean over the Mariana Trench in the Pacific would take over one hour to sink to the bottom.

1 Sixty-five years ago, Americans had more than three times as many recycling projects as they do now.

8 Warner Brothers film studio moguls bought 700 screenplays they never made into movies.

1 The 24 million extra Americans born since 1984 will consume more resources than the whole population of Africa.

8 Over 5,000 new motor vehicles are produced every minute.

1 The percentage of English and Welsh 16-year-olds in sixth-form or further education has doubled in 7 years.

8 Twenty-three thousand oil spills have occurred in Prudhoe Bay, Alaska, since the tundra began being explored for oil in the 1970s.

1 Since World War Two, nearly half the UK's ancient forest has been damaged or destroyed.

8 Only 18 years of production would be required to string a line of Barbie dolls to the moon.

1 Canadian trappers kill as many as 250 wild foxes a day.

8 Three-quarters of Britain's sewage is pumped offshore untreated.

1 Britons together watch 26,000 years of TV a night.

8 Plastic thrown away by Americans every year would fill a queue of 158 supertankers stretching 34 miles.

1 Nearly half of all American children do not live in two-natural-parent families.

8 For every human killed by a shark, 4.5m sharks are killed by humans.

1 Oil spills polluting the oceans each year are the equivalent of 20 major supertanker disasters.

8 Coca-Cola spends approximately $3 billion a year advertising a product that is nearly 100 per cent sugar and water.

1 The English wiped out their wolves 800 years before the French.

8 A rat is estimated to be within 20 feet of every Briton.

1 A Hollywood dog earns more in two days than a typical Haitian does in a year.

8 A keen driver could test-drive a different 1998 car model every Saturday for 14 years.

1 Britons are consuming nearly 4,000 Olympic swimming pools of diluted sugar as 'soft drinks' a year.

8 British gardeners spread on average over £1 million-worth of pesticides a week.

1 Half the three billion people in Asia are under 25.

8 The average car has 100,000 components.

1 There are only 1,200 lynx left in the world.

8 Pure water leaking from British plumbing would fill more than 1,500 Olympic swimming pools every day.

1 If atoms were used for digits in digital storage, all the approximately 24 million different books in the world could fit into a grain of sand.

8 Satellites circling 20,000 km above the Earth are used to position buildings' foundations to an accuracy of plus or minus 25 millimetres.

1 One hundred pairs of royal eagles are estimated to be left in France.

8 The flour used at a pizza restaurant chain for one year's pizzas weighed as much as seven jumbo jets.

1 Reduced 25,000 times, the contents of the *Encyclopaedia Britannica* would fit on to the head of a pin.

8 Placed end to end, trees felled by humans worldwide during the Christmas–New Year holiday season would easily stretch to the moon.

1 The British Isles are surrounded by an estimated 100,000 shipwrecks.

8 In Los Angeles, 12 million people drive 8 million cars over 100 million vehicle-miles a day, using half as much fuel as the entire former Soviet Union.

1 The world's computers use as much electricity as Brazil.

8 A day's German steel production could build 22 Eiffel Towers.

1 Between 3,000 and 5,000 barn owls
are killed on UK roads every year.

8 Child gunshot deaths in the USA outnumber
US battle casualties in Vietnam.

1 Earth's insects weigh 12 times as
much as the human race.

8 Britons spend twice as much as
Swedes on defence, and three
times as much as Germans.

1 A year's discarded motor tyres could stack
10,000 kilometres into outer space, or 500
times higher than a cruising Concorde.

8 British bicycles are stolen at a rate of 200 an hour.

1 American viewers watch 3.5 million years of TV commercials per year.

8 Britain's capital city has one ice rink per 1.1 million residents.

1 Jet planes use nearly a third of all engine fuel.

8 Twice as much is spent on personal computers as on consumer books.

1 Henry the Eighth had an average of five enemies a day executed.

8 Cockroaches can run at the human equivalent of 200 mph.

1 Canada spends more than half as much again on education as Britain.

8 136,000 sacrificial human skulls were found by Spaniards beneath the temple of Quetzalcoatl in Mexico City.

1 Every year, at least 44,000 endangered albatrosses are drowned by biting Japanese tuna-fishing hooks as they are put out.

8 It would take nearly four supertanker loads of grain to raise Chinese annual beer consumption by one bottle per adult.

1 On average, every five miles of British road sees a badger killed each year.

8 If all the vehicles towed away from Greater London's streets in a year by police were tightly parked, they would fill 130 soccer fields.

1 A year brings 19,500 tourists per manatee in Florida.

8 Britain's roadside verges represent a potential nature reserve the size of Berkshire.

1 Seven million square kilometres of Earth's habitable tropical and temperate land is still wilderness – an area almost the size of Brazil.

8 Building a typical American dream home generates seven tons of construction rubbish.

1 Almost a third of the petrol that goes through a two-stroke outboard motor is spewed into the water.

8 Britain's police cars have 54 accidents a day.

1 In the next three years, Britons will eat a 30-storey stack of sandwiches the size of a rugby field.

8 Three months' worth of British telephone books weigh as much as the Leaning Tower of Pisa.

1 British Telecom's scrap tyres each year would form a column 44 times the height of the London BT Tower.

8 A year's recycled BT rental telephones yielded 14 kilograms of gold.

1 A 30-minute telephone call from London to Manchester uses 330 times less energy than the equivalent car journey.

8 Replacing one in 10 car trips with a phone call could conserve half the production of Britain's biggest oil refinery.

1 In the next year, human settlements will emit enough carbon dioxide to fill an 80 million-kilometre queue of Hindenburg airships from here to the planet Mars.

8 Five and a half days and nights of the water going over the Niagara Falls would be required to make a year's motor vehicles.

1 Enough energy-saving lamps have been installed worldwide to save about 18 large coal-fired power plants.

8 Potatoes are 104 times more expensive when eaten in the form of crisps.

1 If the desert area added to the Sahara desert since 1940 had been covered with solar power stations, it could power the whole world.

8 Although air travel is expected to nearly double, nobody is paid to protect the skies from airliners.

1 Platinum dust (from engines) is six times more abundant in the streets of West London than in platinum mines.

8 Consumption of bottled water has tripled since tap water was privatized.

1 For every tiger poached in India, there are roughly eight to ten leopards killed.

8 The electricity used by one car factory could power 40 railway trains.

1 World commercial vehicles would stack to the moon.

8 The top dozen concrete-pouring countries alone produce enough concrete to build twin office towers at least 72 miles high.

1 Frogs have been thriving on Earth for around 1,500 times longer than humans.

8 Researchers believe a human brain can make more connections at one time than all the phone callers in the USA in the past decade.

1 Annual crops of fruit and vegetables and other foods from sunny Spain and Italy have been sprayed with pesticides weighing as much as 28 Eiffel Towers.

8 Pablo Picasso averaged 8.7 handmade pictures every day of his 75-year adult life.

1 The nearest planet to Earth in our galaxy, the Milky Way, is 7,700 million million miles away.

8 Kids spend 70 times as much on computer games as rock guitars.

1 Five American children an hour are injured with a supermarket trolley.

8 Britons eat more than a million tonnes of tinned food a year, or a stack of cans about 170,000 miles high.

1 For every English subject Queen Elizabeth I had, Queen Elizabeth II has more than eleven.

8 It would take a typical London stage-play 118 years to reach the audience of one TV soap.

1 A day's UK sales of colour TVs could make 27 stacks as tall as the Blackpool Tower.

8 Women earn less than half what men earn for Hollywood acting parts.

1 If there were only one British driver, and that driver drove all the miles driven by British cars in a year, he or she would go round the world 12 million times.

8 Lethal pieces of space junk in orbit could double in number within 14 years.

1 A potato has more chromosomes per cell than a human being.

8 A million tons of pulsar stars would fit into a thimble.

1 Britain's domestic cats are believed to have killed 20,000,000 birds.

8 Britons eat 547.5 million cans of baked beans a year.

1 Paper envelopes made each year by the NatWest bank would stack 181 kilometres high, or almost 1,000 times higher than the NatWest Tower in London.

8 Your intestines are longer than a typical sitting room (7.5 metres).

1 In the next three nights, more than 80 UFO sightings will be reported.

8 Ninety-five per cent of animal species do not have a backbone.

1 The moon of Jupiter called Io is pemanently erupting due to its hundreds of volcanoes.

8 A square kilometre of sea contains half a tonne of gold.

1 Over 11% of the world's population now owns an iPod.

8 Copies of the biggest-selling single hit of all time, Bing Crosby's *White Christmas*, would stack 90 kilometres high.

1 In 1997, *The Simpsons* broke the record for the longest prime-time animated TV show. It also holds the record for the highest number of guest stars in a TV series.

8 *Blue Peter* is the longest running children's TV show, having first been broadcast in 1958.

1 More than twice as many people watched the World Cup soccer final in Rio de Janeiro as watched it at Wembley, England.

8 Brazil has scored nearly three times as many goals as England in World Cup soccer matches.

1 A champion long-distance swimmer can cover 25 kilometres in five hours and 21 minutes – the equivalent of walking speed.

8 The maximum break of 147 has been scored six times in ranking snooker tournaments.

1 One of the biggest races in the world is a skiing event, the Vasalopp in Norway, with over 12,000 men and women competing.

8 The oldest ski ever found is 2,500 years old.

1 A shinty pitch in the Scottish Highlands is 170 yards long. Shinty is a hockey-like game.

8 The Spanish are the world champions of roller hockey with a total of 15 gold medals, 12 silver and 7 bronze.

1 A world speed-skating champion averages 87 kilometres an hour in the 2000 m event.

8 Champion powerlifter Karl Sanger can raise 333 kilograms on each arm. The average weight of a man in the UK is around 80 kilograms.

1 The highest average speed ever obtained in a powerboat race is 149 kilometres an hour.

8 Drag-racing cars can reach over 300 miles an hour in about five seconds.

1 The longest race in the world is 32,000 nautical miles (the Whitbread Round the World Race for yachts).

8 TV's *Neighbours*, which has been running for over 324 months, was originally cancelled after only six.

1 *Newsround* has appeared on BBC children's TV over 5,000 times, and tape-recordings of it could be played round-the-clock for 36 days.